BEAT IT!

Group percussion for beginners by Evelyn Glennie & Paul Cameron

AFRICAN DANCES

Complete resource pack for group use including CD

African Dances

Inserts: CD, Piano scores

© 1997 by Faber Music Ltd
First published in 1997 by Faber Music Ltd
Bloomsbury House
74–77 Great Russell Street
London WC1B 3DA
Illustrations by John Levers
Cover design by S & M Tucker
Printed in England by Caligraving Ltd
All rights reserved

ISBN10: 0-571-51778-1
EAN13: 978-0-571-51778-7

To buy Faber Music publications or to find out about the full range of titles available
please contact your local music retailer or Faber Music sales enquiries:

Faber Music Ltd, Burnt Mill, Elizabeth Way, Harlow, Essex CM20 2HX
Tel: +44 (0)1279 82 89 82   Fax: +44 (0)1279 82 89 83
sales@fabermusic.com   fabermusic.com

Introduction

How to use this book

This book and CD present four African dances which can be used by both classroom teachers and percussion specialists. Together, they are an extremely versatile resource for music making.

Our aim is to give an approach to discovering rhythm and how it can be used to build up performances. We seek to encourage flexible teaching techniques by matching instruments available to individuals and groups at many levels of musical understanding. The following guidelines explain how to use the book and CD.

How to use the Rhythm Accompaniment Workshops

Workshop learning is at the core of *Beat it!*, enabling students to develop a rhythmic foundation and vocabulary. The Rhythm Accompaniment Workshops offer a step-by-step approach to the *use* of rhythm, primarily through listening. Treat them as versatile 'workstations'. For each dance, they can be used individually or together to lead a group through the simple skills essential for understanding rhythm and how it can be used in performance. Each dance has three such workshops, developing rhythmic accompaniment ideas to add to the instrumental parts and thus build complete performances. Use them to give rhythmic backing to the dances using hand-held percussion instruments, vocalising, movement and body percussion. The techniques explored are effective with small groups or a full class. Each workshop creates a complete accompaniment which can be used separately, or along with one or both of the other two to build and layer rhythmic accompaniments.

Altogether, these twelve workshops cover many musical topics and constitute a substantial contribution to a music curriculum. We recommend working through them in the order given. Use of the ideas and skills presented in this book in other songs, dances, tunes and with other instruments is encouraged and highly recommended.

How to use the Instrument Workshops

These workshops give the technical and practical skills necessary to perform on the instruments referred to in the Rhythm Accompaniment Workshops. It is important that percussion instruments are correctly held and played if rhythms natural to them are to sound and 'feel' good. Tips and techniques are given to enable students to get the best results from the instruments.

Use these sections alongside the Rhythm Accompaniment Workshops to develop particular instrumental skills required by students within the group. Each session should include work on both rhythm and instrumental skills. The Instrument Workshops may also be used as starting points for further projects, encouraging the group to learn other skills.

How to use the music

Each song is an arrangement of traditional African tunes that can be played on tuned and untuned percussion instruments. Melody instruments – for example, recorder, violin – can be included if available. Scores with piano parts and chord symbols are provided as a separate insert, while the melody lines are included within the main book. Where permission is specifically given you may photocopy the parts for your own overhead projector or classroom use only. Try the following:

- Perform Part 1 as a solo melody on a xylophone, glockenspiel or other melodic instrument.

- Perform Parts 1 and 2 as a duet (Part 2 is an easier beginner's part). Note: *Rainbow Nation* uses just a single melody part.

- Perform solo or duet, with piano accompaniment. This is given in each score with chord symbols so that guitar and bass accompaniment can also be added to form a band.

- Perform any of the above with the rhythm accompaniments developed in the workshops. The workshops contain several different projects for each dance (see *How to use the Rhythm Accompaniment Workshops*).

- Perform as solo, duet, or ensemble with the CD backing (see *How to use the CD*).

How to use the CD

The CD can be used in two ways, first, as a backing track when learning or performing the solo and duet parts on tuned percussion instruments. This could be a stand-alone backing or in addition to piano, bass, guitar and the rhythm accompaniments developed in the workshops. Secondly, every example given in the Rhythm Accompaniment Workshops is recorded for demonstration purposes.

When working with the Rhythm Accompaniment Workshops, observe the following procedure to encourage the habit and importance of listening skills:

- Listen to the dance several times in its complete version to familiarise the group with the material to be used.

- Use the CD when indicated in the text.

- Listen to an example several times before asking the group to join in with it. They can then copy and learn it independently of the CD.

- Make listening and playing equally important.

- At the end of the session, listen again to the dance in its complete version so that the group can hear its work in context.

- Now experiment with different performances using CD backing tracks and live instruments according to the skills and instrument resources available. Encourage the students to record these where possible.

- Complete CD contents are listed on page 48.

Learning the tunes

Playing position

- Ensure that the tuned percussion instrument is the correct height for good playing posture. Playing melodies is easier and learning quicker if the performer is comfortable and relaxed. The forearms and sticks should be roughly parallel to the floor. Only sit on the floor to play tuned percussion if a cushion is available; players should also be encouraged to keep a straight back.

- Look at the full pitch range of the piece, and stand so that the body and playing-position are central to the highest and lowest notes.

- Stand with the feet comfortably apart so that the body can rotate at the waist and the weight of the body can move on to each leg in turn. This should give flexible movement up and down the keyboard across the full pitch range of the piece.

Sticking choices (use of left and right hands)

- Sticking choices are often overlooked at the early stages when learning melodies. It is important to understand that good sticking choices result in improved pitch-reading accuracy and general melodic fluency. Try to encourage the use of the weaker hand within a coordinated approach to sticking choices.

- In the simplest terms, having played one note with the right hand the next note has the sticking choice of another right hand or a left hand. Obvious, but given that melodies are directional up and down the keyboard, incremental sticking choices through the melody become fundamental to successful reading.

- Thus, playing melodies well on a tuned percussion instrument relies as much on sticking choices as a melody on a recorder, for example, does on fingering patterns.

Getting started

Snare drum pupils graduating to tuned percussion are often brought up with the rule of 'hand-to-hand' sticking (alternating left hand and right hand in strict succession). This is good for developing equal dexterity in each hand but not particularly relevant to the sticking choices required when learning melodies. As an introduction to tuned percussion, first try playing a 'melody' on a drum, as follows:

- Listen to the full performance of any one African dance on the CD a number of times to hear and understand the shape of the melody. Hear also how the melody fits with the accompaniment. Describe and discuss.

- Counting aloud, listen to the CD backing and clap the rhythm of the melody to understand how counting and rhythm fit together.

- When comfortable and relaxed start to play the rhythm of the melody on a drum. First use whatever sticking seems natural. Play a number of times to become relaxed with playing the rhythm. Try using this as a warm-up exercise or as a means of encouraging the weaker hand.

- At the drum try to think through which sticking would work with the melody. Remember that there is a free choice of sticking at a drum whereas at a tuned percussion instrument there are the considerations of melodic direction, shape and fluency.

- In the same way that we do not cross hands at the drum, try to avoid this possibility when working out sticking for a melody. Two consecutive right or left hands are acceptable.

- Develop the idea of sticking patterns that fit melodic patterns.

- Finally, take these sticking patterns to the tuned percussion instrument and work them into the melodic patterns, slowly, one pattern at a time.

- Build up the melody in stages but don't always start at the beginning. With *Mavuto Megamix*, for example, it is fun to change the order of the six short tunes.

- When all parts of the melody are comfortable at the same tempo then practise playing the whole melody with CD backing.

- Work at playing the piece without stopping as a *skill* in itself.

There's more to learning melodies than correct notes

- This is where learning to *perform* starts.

- The written page is a set of instructions to be interpreted by a performer and communicated to an audience.

- Interpretation is individual reading, but communication is a group activity. At all levels and standards try to encourage *performance* so that this becomes a natural part of music making.

- Make regular use of performance as a feature of all your music-making sessions so that the habit of communication is encouraged. Do not wait until the end of term or for a special occasion to perform but include it as part of each lesson or practice session, even if it is just two bars of music. Always imagine an audience in the room.

- Dynamics are an essential part of performance. In *Beat it!*, we have decided not to be prescriptive about the use of dynamics, but to invite creativity within the group. Pupils should be encouraged to discuss the use of dynamics and experiment with a range of performance outcomes.

national curriculum guidelines

Overview

African Dances will extend pupils' musical experience and knowledge, and develop their appreciation of the richness of African music. It gives pupils the opportunity to:

- control sounds made by the voice, hands, body, hand-held percussion instruments and tuned percussion
- perform and develop an awareness of others
- explore a range of resources
- communicate musical ideas to others

African Dances also encourages pupils to use sounds and respond to music through:

- listening with concentration and attention to detail and understanding through exploring, identifying and developing musical ideas
- 'internalising' rhythmic shapes and percussive sounds in the Rhythm Accompaniment Workshops
- performance which allows the pupils to recognise, distinguish and discriminate between separate musical elements

African Dances can develop a pupils' understanding and enjoyment of music. The elements of accompaniment workshop and performance bring together requirements from performing, composing, listening and appraising as specified in the National Curriculum.

Assessment

Satisfactory achievement will have the following qualities:

Key Stage 1
Pupils play pieces and workshop accompaniments with confidence and awareness of pulse. They will explore, select and order sounds. Pupils respond to pieces recognising repetition and rhythmic shapes.

Key Stage 2
Pupils perform accurately and confidently, making expressive use of rhythmic shape and showing awareness of phrase. They maintain independent rhythmic and instrumental lines with awareness of the other performers in the workshop

group. They select and combine appropriate resources, use musical structures and symbols when performing and communicate musical ideas.

Pupils begin to recognise how music is affected by place. They listen with attention to detail and describe and compare music from different traditions, using a musical vocabulary.

Key Stage 3
Pupils perform individual parts with confidence and control, and interpret the mood or feel of the piece. They show awareness of other performers and fit their own part within the whole. They develop musical ideas within structures, using different textures and percussive sounds.

Pupils respond to the pieces, identifying conventions used within different styles and traditions. They use a musical vocabulary appropriately.

Exceptional performance may be identified as:
Pupils who direct others in group performances and/or perform a solo part in a group, demonstrating a sense of ensemble and recognising when to take the lead and when to support others. They develop musical ideas exploring structures and exploiting a range of resources.

Pupils identify resources used in *African Dances*. They identify continuity and change within a range of musical traditions from African culture, making connections between the music and its cultural context.

traditional african percussion

The four dances use a variety of African percussion techniques and sounds, and it is hoped the following background information will be valuable.

Mavuto Megamix

The foot stomping techniques developed in *Mavuto Megamix* can imitate the traditional use and sound of a *stamped pit* (log drum): a hole is dug in the ground and covered with a rough wooden lid which is then struck by various implements to create a percussive rhythm. Sticks, gourds and bamboo tubes are all used for stamping or occasionally played against the player's thigh. The tubes are of varying length and diameter, and are played with both ends open, or one end closed to produce notes of different pitch. Occasionally they are used in combination to produce a melody.

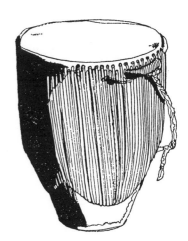

Large drum, Central Africa

Omusambwa Kwetsingoma

Drums are widespread throughout Africa. Usually carved out of solid logs of wood, they are sometimes made from strips of wood bound together by iron hoops. Earthenware vessels are also used for drum shells, the

Sakara, Nigeria

Carved drum with lizard skins, E. Africa

Sakara drum of the of the Yoruba, Nigeria being a typical example: the shell is about 10 inches in diameter and 1½ inches deep. The large gourd and calabash are also both used for drum shells, with tins and light oil drums occasionally used as a substitute. Drum shape is as varied as size, with some large drums over one metre tall and up to eighty centimetres in diameter. Use of drumsticks is common,

Kalengo, or 'talking' drum, Ghana

with the drum often played with hand and stick allowing the cupped hand, palm, palm and fingers, or base of the palm in different positions to affect tone quality and pitch. One of the most interesting double skinned drums found in Africa is the *Kalengo* ('talking' or hour glass-shaped) drum. The *Dagomba* people of Ghana have a system to rank the musicians who play the *Kalengo* drum. The qualifications for leadership are, firstly, a knowledge of *Dagomba* literature and the traditional history of the area, secondly, a sweet singing voice and, finally, a supple wrist to play the drum!

Celebration

The string rattle is made of small hard objects such as teeth, hooves, shells and seeds laced or bunched together. With the

Gourd rattles, Africa

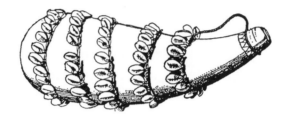

Cowrie shell gourd rattle, Africa

Wood rattle, Africa

instrument shaken or strung from the ankle, leg, arm, or neck of the dancer it can emphasise dance rhythms. Rattles are made using the ears of the springbok or dry hide: the ears, which are sewn together, are partly filled with small pieces of ostrich egg shell or dried berries which act as rattling pieces. Bushman bells consist of large hollow balls made of dry hide, which contain a number of small pebbles. The 'bells' are fastened to the shoulders or upper arms and shaken with a sudden jerk to the tempo of the dance.

Rainbow Nation

African drums are played singly, in pairs or in larger ensembles, grouped and graded according to tone and pitch. One such arrangement is a set of fifteen *entenga* drums of the Kabaka (king) of Uganda. The drums are tuned to definite pitches and are used for playing melodies similar to those played on the xylophone. Among smaller sets are the *namaddu* drum chime of the *Lango*

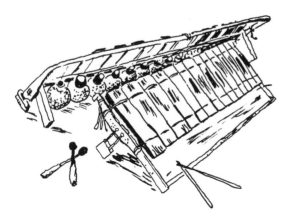

Marimba, South Africa, showing resonating gourds beneath the keys

people. Tuned drums are also found among the *Digo* people in Kenya and the *Zaramo* people in Tanzania.

Xylophones and marimbas are played as solo instruments or in small ensembles. Larger ensembles, known locally as *timbila* bands with as many as thirty xylophones, are found among the *Chopi* people in Mozambique. Traditionally in Uganda a number of performers will play one instrument. Three players play the *amadinda*, with up to six performers playing the *akadinda*. They are usually accompanied by a rhythm section made up of drums and rattles, bells, castanets or percussion sticks.

mavuto megamix

Mavuto Megamix is an arrangement of traditional folk tunes from Malawi. There are six short tunes with each identified by a letter from the word Mavuto. The piano score of *Mavuto Megamix* (*see insert 'Piano Scores'*) joins all six tunes together into a longer piece. It also includes chord symbols for guitar, etc. For parts see page 35.

 CD 1 *Mavuto Megamix* – whole piece, full performance

Using Pitch

The two parts are to be played on tuned percussion or melody instruments or sung. Part 1 is a melody line, to be played on a xylophone, glockenspiel or other melody instrument. Part 2 is an easier, beginner's part which functions as a bass line. It can be played lower down on the same instrument or on a second tuned instrument. It may also be transposed to the timpani by a more experienced player, or a bass melody instrument (eg. bass guitar or cello) using the bass clef part on page 37.

Parts 1 & 2 for *Mavuto Megamix* – see page 35.

Learn Parts 1 & 2 with the group. CD tracks 2-21 will help you do this.

 CD 2 - 7 (Parts 1 & 2 with backing): the six tunes separately M - A - V - U - T - O. *Use for listening before learning Parts 1 & 2, and as a backing for the rhythm and instrument workshops.*

 CD 8 - 13 (Part 2 with backing): the six tunes separately M - A - V - U - T - O.

 CD 14 (Part 2 with backing): the whole piece. *Use as a backing when learning or performing Part 1 and for listening to Part 2.*

 CD 15 - 20 (Part 1 with backing): the six tunes separately M - A - V - U - T - O.

 CD 21 (Part 1 with backing): the whole piece. *Use as a backing when learning or performing Part 2 and for listening to Part 1.*

 CD 22 *Mavuto Megamix* – whole piece, full backing only *Use as a backing when learning or Parts 1 & 2 together, or for a full performance of the whole piece.*

RHYTHM ACCOMPANIMENT WORKSHOPS

Rhythm accompaniment to *Mavuto Megamix* uses co-ordination and independence of hands, feet and voice. In traditional African dances, this is clapping, foot stomping and singing. We begin by using simple and familiar rhythmic patterns.

rhythm 1
ACCOMPANIMENT
WORKSHOP

WORKSHOP 1: VOICES

To copy rhythmic patterns with the voice, use phonetics. These are nonsense words that can recreate the sound of percussion instruments.

● Play the full performance of *Mavuto Megamix* (CD 1) and encourage the students to listen to the eighth note/quaver rhythmic pattern of the accompaniment. Vocalise the phonetics 'Gee ya Ka Ka' to this pattern with the backing band on CD. Use a comfortable speaking voice:

 CD 23

gee-ya ka ka gee-ya ka ka

● Make the 'Gee' sound long and join it to 'ya', making 'Gee-ya' one word. Practise this.

● Make the 'Ka Ka' sounds short and hard.

● Learn to relax with phonetics by vocalising the following patterns with the full performance track on CD (CD 1). Try changing the phonetic pattern every four bars:

 CD 24

a) ‖: *gee-ya ka ka gee ya ka ka* :‖

b) ‖: *ka ka gee-ya ka ka gee-ya* :‖

c) ‖:*-ya ka ka gee-ya ka ka gee-*:‖

d) ‖: *ka gee-ya ka ka gee-ya ka* :‖

● Now ask the group to invent and experiment with their own vocal sounds that match the eighth note/quaver feel of the accompaniment. For example, try vocalising 'Mee ya Ma Ma' in the patterns already established.

rhythm 2
ACCOMPANIMENT WORKSHOP

WORKSHOP 2: CO-ORDINATION OF HANDS AND FEET WITH VOICE

● Stand up! Listen to *Mavuto Megamix* (CD 1) and vocalise phonetics with the full performance track on CD to the quaver/eighth note rhythmic pattern of the accompaniment, as in Rhythm Accompaniment Workshop 1. Now use one hand to copy the vocal patterns by playing onto the body. Try clapping, tapping, or slapping the thigh. At all times keep vocalising the phonetics.

CD 25

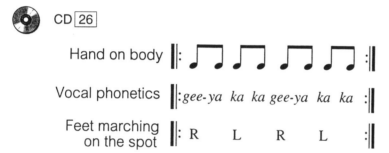

Hand on body

Vocal phonetics ‖: gee-ya ka ka gee-ya ka ka :‖

● When this is comfortable, add a relaxed movement from right to left foot on the spot, one step to two hand movements:

CD 26

Hand on body

Vocal phonetics ‖: gee-ya ka ka gee-ya ka ka :‖

Feet marching on the spot ‖: R   L   R   L :‖

● Keep the hand playing and feet moving in time with the backing track then make the vocal phonetics silent, but continue to think its sound and rhythmic shape.

● Now make the hand pattern silent, but continue to feel its pulse.

● With the feet still moving from right to left, introduce the following new vocal phonetics in time with the feet:

CD 27

Silent pulse

Vocal phonetics ‖: gung ka   gung   ka :‖

Feet marching on the spot ‖: R   L   R   L :‖

● Make 'Gung' a long relaxed sound and emphasise the sound 'Ka' within the pattern.

● Finally, use one hand to copy the 'Ka' sound in the vocal pattern by playing onto the body as before.

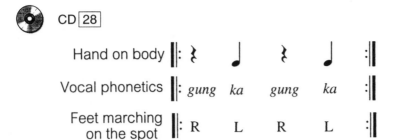

● Use these hand and feet patterns as an accompaniment to *Mavuto Megamix*.

WORKSHOP 3: INDEPENDENCE OF HANDS, FEET AND VOICE

A 'drum kit' can be recreated by using hands, feet and voice. Here are two examples to be explored with the workshop group whilst listening to *Mavuto Megamix*:

Each example has five individual parts that together contain material to build hand, feet and voice independence:

    Part 1: Hand on body

    Part 2: Vocal pattern 1

    Part 3: Vocal pattern 2

    Part 4: Hand on body

    Part 5: Feet marching on spot

● Begin by asking each student to choose and 'play' different pairs of lines together.

● Once hands and feet are co-ordinated a vocalised pattern can be added.

- Individual and group duet vocalising can then be introduced using the two vocal lines together.

- Alternatively, five individuals or groups can take a single rhythmic or vocal part and perform the whole pattern together. Encourage an awareness of ensemble.

- Perform, and enjoy the performance!

- All these rhythm combinations can be used to accompany the six tunes that together build *Mavuto Megamix*. Once the students are confident with the material they may choose to mix the order of the six tunes (and letters), to make new nonsense words and to improve their melodic fluency. Use the first drum kit pattern in Rhythm Accompaniment Workshop 3 for tunes M, A, T and O and the second for tunes V and U. Performed in this way, we are capturing the singing, clapping and foot stomping of these traditional folk tunes from Malawi.

INSTRUMENT WORKSHOP

All the African dances in this book can be accompanied by the three instruments that together form a pop drum kit – **cymbal**, **snare drum** and **bass drum**. The simple rhythmic patterns explored in *Mavuto Megamix* are good examples:

 CD 29 & 30

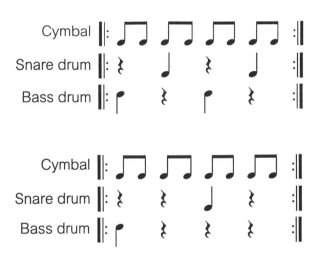

Explore alternative instruments and techniques that recreate the sound characteristics of this pattern.

- The quaver/eighth note rhythm of the cymbal can be played on a **triangle**. Practise the 'Gee ya Ka Ka' rhythm used in *Mavuto Megamix* to help create a good rhythmic shape.

- The triangle is held in the left hand, whilst the right hand holds a metal beater, or vice versa.

- The beater is held between the thumb and the first joint of the index finger. This finger is bent underneath the beater.

● The strokes are played using the wrist and these two fingers.

● Simple rhythmic improvisation can be encouraged by the creative use of 'open' and 'closed' strokes. These are made using the hand that holds the triangle:

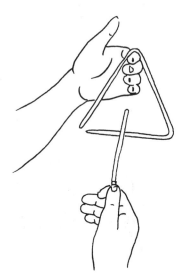

Open stroke (o)

The triangle should hang from the index finger of the left hand, or from a small loop of string around the triangle and held with the index finger. The fingers are held together and curved at right angles to the hand. Use this open stroke with the 'gee' sound.

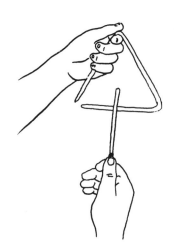

Closed stroke (+)

This is used for all other vocal sounds. The fingers and thumb are clenched around the triangle to dampen the sound.

All strokes are played with the beater. Experiment with where it strikes the triangle to vary the sound quality. Open strokes will sound louder than closed strokes.

● Simple rhythmic improvisation can be encouraged by the creative use of open and closed strokes.

● Here are four examples using open and closed strokes with their vocal pattern:

 CD 31

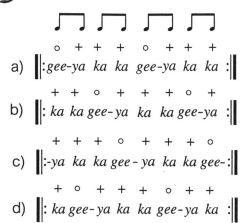

Similar rhythms can be played on the **suspended cymbal**.

This can be played with a wooden stick held in a similar way to the triangle beater. The other hand allows open and closed strokes. It is useful to keep the second finger against the underneath of the cymbal at all times to prevent it moving around too much.

 CD 32

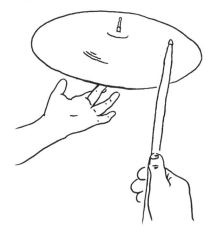 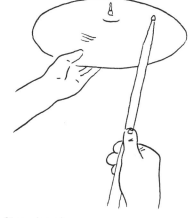

Open stroke   *Closed stroke*

- Instruments played with the hands can also be used, such as the **shaker**. Again, the 'Gee ya Ka Ka' vocal phonetics can be used, or the rhythmic patterns developed later in *Omusambwa Kwetsingoma*.

- A **snare drum** can play the strong 'Ka' sound as part of the 'Gung ka Gung ka' rhythm explored in *Mavuto Megamix*. Play the drum head in the centre with a wooden stick. Alternatively two sticks can be struck together or a whip sound used, created by slapping two strips of wood together.

- A **tambourine** can be used to recreate the snare drum part.

The tambourine is normally held flat with one hand and struck with the palm of the other hand, although players may be encouraged to experiment with other ways of holding and playing the instrument. Try to discover how many different sounds you can make with it.

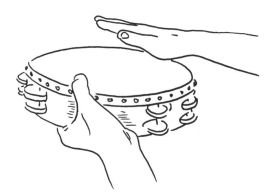 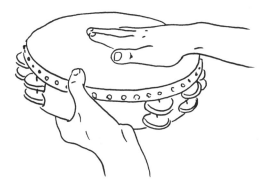

mavuto megamix

● A **bass drum** can be used to play the 'Gung' sound as part of the 'Gung-ka' rhythm. The bass drum could be any pitched drum lower than the snare sound, played using a softer stick. It may also be a hand held drum played with one stick in the other hand. Make this a resonant sound.

● Any **large drum** can be slapped with the fingers of one hand to play the bass drum part. Strike the drum with the fingertips removing them promptly to allow the sound to sustain.

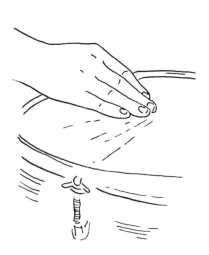

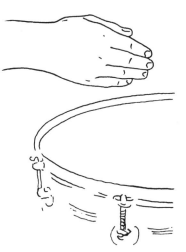

omusambwa kwetsingoma

Omusambwa Kwetsingoma translates to 'the spirit of percussion'. This arrangement combines four short tunes typical of those found in Kenya, Ghana and Nigeria. The piano score uses all four tunes in a single piece, but in a more sophisticated way than with *Mavuto Megamix*. It also includes chord symbols for guitar, etc. For parts see page 38.

 CD 33 *Omusambwa Kwetsingoma* – whole piece, full performance

Using Pitch

The two parts are to be played on tuned percussion or melody instruments or sung. Part 1 is a melody line, to be played on a xylophone, glockenspiel or other melody instrument. Part 2 is an easier, beginner's part which functions as a bass line. It can be played lower down on the same instrument or on a second tuned instrument. It may also be transposed to the timpani by a more experienced player, or a bass melody instrument (eg. bass guitar or cello) using the bass clef part on page 42.

Parts 1 & 2 for *Omusambwa Kwetsingoma* – see page 38.

Learn Parts 1 & 2 with the group. CD tracks 34 - 47 will help you do this.

 CD 34 - 37 (Parts 1 & 2 with backing): the four tunes separately.
Use for listening before learning Parts 1 & 2, and as a backing for the rhythm and instrument workshops.

 CD 38 - 41 (Part 2 with backing): the four tunes separately.

 CD 42 (Part 2 with backing): the whole piece.
Use as a backing when learning or performing Part 1 and for listening to Part 2.

 CD 43 - 46 (Part 1 with backing): the four tunes separately.

 CD 47 (Part 1 with backing): the whole piece.
Use as a backing when learning or performing Part 2 and for listening to Part 1.

 CD 48 *Omusambwa Kwetsingoma* – whole piece, full backing only.
Use as a backing when learning or Parts 1 & 2, or for a full performance of the whole piece.

RHYTHM ACCOMPANIMENT WORKSHOPS

In *Omusambwa Kwetsingoma* we explore pulse and its subdivisions. The key to this is the use of the shaker, known locally as the *Chakacha* (pronounced cha-kar-cha). The starting point is the most familiar pulse in our everyday lives, the tick-tock of a clock, so encourage a relaxed and natural feel.

WORKSHOP 1: PULSE

The key concept in this workshop is **pulse** and its relationship to **beat** and **tempo** (or speed).

- Ask the students to find and clap their own pulse (heart beat). Use this opportunity to discuss **pulse**, and a regular **beat**. Discuss how this can drive music along.

- Listen for some time to the tick-tock of a clock or a metronome set to 60 beats per minute and become relaxed and confident with its **tempo**. Then listen to *Omusambwa Kwetsingoma* on the CD and encourage the students to become familiar with its strong, regular **beat**.

- Move your body from side to side, on to the right foot and then the left foot, in time with the **pulse**.

- Now, some in the workshop group can pick up a shaker and play a simple rhythm with four movements to each **pulse**, by causing the contents to move back and forth inside the instrument. Refer to the shaker instrument workshop on page 24.

- Develop your listening to hear a smooth and relaxed sound. Play the rhythm for a long time, preferably in a group with the eyes shut. There is a tendency to use too much energy making the small movements involved, so encourage a relaxed and natural feel.

WORKSHOP 2: VOICE PATTERNS

To copy rhythmic patterns with the voice, use phonetics. These can be the words *Omusambwa* and *Kwetsingoma* used together to recreate the shaker rhythm.

- Vocalise these phonetics as a whisper whilst also playing the shaker rhythm. Alternatively, divide the workshop group into two, with one group playing or clapping the shaker rhythm, while the second group vocalises the phonetics:

 CD 49

Shaker rhythm:
Vocal phonetics: o -mus -sam -bwa kwet - sin-go - ma   o -mu -sam - bwa kwet -sin-go - ma

When these phonetics are familiar and relaxed it is time to begin developing voice patterns. Listen to the full performance of *Omusambwa Kwetsingoma* several times (CD 33). Encourage the group to think about how they are listening and what they are listening for, as follows:

a) First, listen to the shape of the melody. It should be quite easy to hear the pitch going up and down.

b) Next, ask the workshop group to listen for a different quality in the melody. They may be able to guess that it has rhythm.

c) Finally, listen to how the rhythm of the melody fits with the shaker rhythm accompaniment. The shaker provides a rhythmic framework which supports the rhythm of the melody.

● You can develop different voice patterns as accompaniments to the melody. These can be used as frameworks which will help make the rhythm of a melody become more comfortable and relaxed and will also help when learning to play the melodies.

● The following example shows some voice patterns which can be used as frameworks to help support the rhythm of each melody. You can learn these along with each of the four short melodies used in the arrangement of *Omusambwa Kwetsingoma*.

CD 50

omusambwa kwetsingoma

There is no need at this stage to introduce the written example to the workshop group. Learning is by listening and repetition of the voice patterns.

● Listen to each melody and each voice pattern many times. When the workshop group are relaxed and comfortable try to encourage them to join in vocalising the voice patterns.

● Do not use a particular pitch when vocalising, but a comfortable speaking voice to make the sounds smooth and relaxed. Do not worry about diction but allow the sounds to become an accompaniment rhythm. Feel free to allow the voice to emphasise the shape of the rhythm if this feels natural.

● When each voice pattern is relaxed, confident and consistent, try to encourage each performer to play the shaker rhythm and do the voice patterns at the same time.

● The workshop group should invent and experiment with their own vocal sounds that match these voice patterns.

● Perform *Omusambwa Kwetsingoma* with the full backing, using voice patterns and shaker accompaniment (CD 48). Try creating new voice patterns and sounds that match these rhythms.

WORKSHOP 3: 'BASS LINE' RHYTHM

The **drum** is often used as an accompaniment instrument. A large drum that gives a strong resonant sound is ideal. The performer can use its bass tones to create a 'bass line' which can be added to the voice patterns explored in Rhythm Accompaniment Workshop 2. Refer also to the large drum instrument workshop on p.25.

● The rhythms may appear daunting when written down, but through listening and repetition, and by using the voice patterns, a 'feel' for the rhythm will develop.

● Divide the group into two. One group vocalises one of the voice patterns from Rhythm Accompaniment Workshop 2 whilst maintaining the shaker rhythm. The other group plays the 'bass line' rhythm on a large drum. The key to working together is that the bass line uses the voice pattern as a framework to support the rhythm:

 CD 51

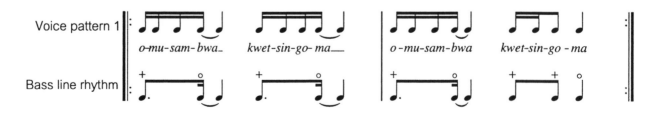

Voice pattern 2
o - mu -sam- bwa____ kwet - sin - go - ma

Bass line rhythm

Voice pattern 3
o - - mu - sam-bwa kwet-sin-go -ma kwet-sin-go -ma

Bass line rhythm

Voice pattern 4
o - mu-sam-bwa kwet - sin - go - ma

Bass line rhythm

- Layer the sounds in the following order:

  a) Group 1 play the shaker pattern.

  b) When comfortable, group 1 vocalise one of the voice patterns.

  c) Group 2 need to be familiar with the large drum. This group should listen to the shaker pattern and voice patterns of group 1.

  d) When comfortable, group 2 play the 'bass line' rhythm to fit with voice pattern.

  e) Try playing all closed strokes (+) first until the players become confident with the rhythm, then introduce the open strokes (o) as shown in the previous example.

- Perform in separate layers, then build up the ensemble. If necessary Group 1 can split into two smaller groups, one playing the shaker rhythm and the other doing the voice patterns.

- When this is relaxed, confident and consistent the bass line performers can begin to improvise with open strokes placed at different places within the rhythmic pattern. This simply gives some freedom to experiment with the placing of open strokes within the bass line rhythm. Individuals within the group can take it in turns to improvise. More experienced performers may wish to improvise with the rhythms. The important rule is to keep listening to group 1. If the improvised rhythm fits with the voice pattern and the shaker rhythm then, for this workshop, it is 'good' improvisation.

- Try to relax with the rhythmic patterns. Communicate a natural rhythmic shape using the open strokes to emphasise this.

omusambwa kwetsingoma

- Devise your own dynamics (louds and softs) with the group and try different ideas.

- Perform, and enjoy the performance!

INSTRUMENT WORKSHOP

When familiar with vocalising rhythmic patterns you may wish to introduce **pitch**, played on a tuned percussion instrument, keyboard, etc. Pitch is the next step to building on the foundations established in the workshop material adding to a framework of rhythm, vocalising and listening. The following example uses the voice patterns of *Omusambwa Kwetsingoma* as illustrated on CD 50 :

- Vocalise, under your breath or aloud, the voice patterns used so far to give a shape to each rhythm (refer to WORKSHOP 2: VOICE PATTERNS on page 18).

- Play the melodies along with the voice patterns.

- Now, add the rhythmic accompaniment of a shaker rhythm. When this is comfortable add the bass line rhythm on a large drum.

- Once this is established and feels comfortable, pitch can also be added to the 'bass line' rhythm, as shown in the following example and illustrated on CD 51 . Again, use voice patterns to set up the shape of the rhythm:

omusambwa kwetsingoma

Ex.5

● Both tuned percussion parts are written in the treble clef for easier reading. The choice of instruments may be left to the performers; it is also possible for both parts to be played on one instrument in different octaves. Refer to USING PITCH on p.17. Also in this workshop, we add the **shaker** and **large drum** to our battery of percussion instruments.

Hold the **shaker** with both hands at a height that feels comfortable, usually chest height, and listen carefully to a steady, regular pulse. Refer to WORKSHOP 1: PULSE on page 18.

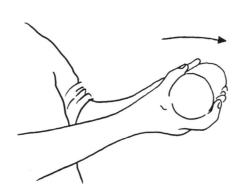

Emphasise the pulse by tossing the contents of the shaker against the inside of the instrument with a quick forwards movement of the arms away from the body.

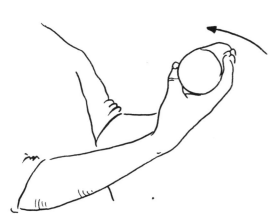

Relax with a light movement of the wrists back towards the body . . .

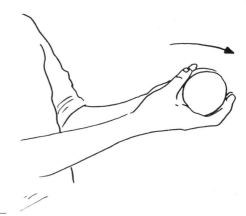

. . . and then away from the body again.

omusambwa kwetsingoma

Mavuto Megamix

This music is copyright. Photocopying is illegal.

Omusambwa Kwetsingoma

4

Celebration

Rainbow Nation

The fourth movement is a quick movement backwards of the arms towards the body. Now the sequence can begin again.

 CD 52 Shaker rhythm

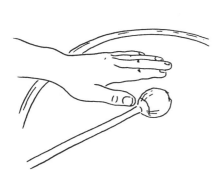

- The **large drum** can be played with a stick in one hand whilst using the other hand to give open or dampened sounds.
- It is best to use a soft headed mallet or the blunt end of a drum stick to strike the drum head.
- The drum can be free-standing, mounted on a stand, or attached by a strap to the performer.
- It is important that the performer is free to move in response to the music.
- There are two different sounds available to the performer:

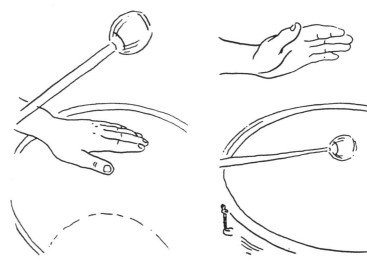

Closed stroke (+)

With one hand placed on the drum head, strike the drum head in the centre with the stick. The dampening hand stays on the drum head throughout the pattern until the next open stroke.

Open stroke (o)

With the dampening hand off the drum, strike the drum head in the centre removing the stick promptly to allow the sound to sustain. Emphasise this stroke within the pattern.

 CD 53 Open and closed drum sounds

omusambwa kwetsingoma

celebration

Celebration in Botswana inspires singing, dancing and clapping. Villagers tie bells to their legs and arms then dance to the same rhythm as the percussion. Everyone joins in with clapping and singing, creating an exciting spectacle of rhythm, pulse and melody. A traditional performance alternates between song and dance with percussion accompaniment. This arrangement joins two songs together with a traditional clapping accompaniment. The piano score includes chord symbols for guitar, etc. For parts see page 44.

 CD 54 *Celebration* – full performance

Using Pitch

The two parts are to be played on tuned percussion or melody instruments or sung. Part 1 is a melody line, to be played on a xylophone, glockenspiel or other melody instrument. Part 2 is an easier, beginner's part which functions as a bass line. It can be played lower down on the same instrument or on a second tuned instrument. It may also be transposed to the timpani by a more experienced player, or a bass melody instrument (eg. bass guitar or cello) using the bass clef part on page 46.

Parts 1 & 2 for *Celebration* – see page 44.

Learn Parts 1 & 2 with the group. CD tracks 55 & 56 will help you do this.

 CD 55 (Part 2 with backing): the whole piece.
Use as a backing when learning or performing Part 1 and for listening to Part 2.

 CD 56 (Part 1 with backing): the whole piece.
Use as a backing when learning or performing Part 2 and for listening to Part 1.

 CD 57 (the whole piece, full backing only with clapping).
Use as a backing when learning or Parts 1 & 2, or for a full performance of the whole piece.

 CD 58 *Celebration* – the whole piece, full backing only without clapping.
Use for a full performance of the whole piece with clapping.

RHYTHM ACCOMPANIMENT WORKSHOPS

Accompaniment to *Celebration* requires the **clapping skills** traditional in African dances. These skills can be encouraged and developed in clapping games. The choice of tempo for clapping games is dictated by how well the group can clap together, whilst remaining relaxed and comfortable. It is important that the clapping is both consistent and continuous.

rhythm
ACCOMPANIMENT
WORKSHOP

WORKSHOP 1: CLAPPING

● Get the group to stand in a circle with their eyes closed. Now ask one student to clap a consistent and continuous pulse to the group. Choose a slow and relaxed tempo. Repeat the pulse many times so that the group become familiar with it.

● Encourage everyone to join in the clapping.

Clapping together as a group is difficult, and tends to break down. It is made easier by introducing a rhythmic shape that the whole group can listen out for. This gives structure to the continuous clapping.

For *Celebration*, the group needs to understand just two rhythmic shapes; either an imaginary △ which is three claps, or an imaginary ⊓ which is two claps.

● Listen to *Celebration* (CD 58). Try thinking in △ and emphasise the first beat of each three.

● Next, listen again to *Celebration* this time thinking in ⊓ . Stress the first of each pair of beats.

● Repeat each rhythmic shape many times so that the clapping becomes relaxed, confident and memorised.

rhythm
ACCOMPANIMENT
WORKSHOP

WORKSHOP 2: MORE CLAPPING

When the feel of rhythmic shapes is secure introduce the open and closed clapping strokes as explained in the instrument workshop on page 30.

For the ⊓ shape use an open sound followed by a closed sound:

 CD 59

```
   o  +  o  +  o  +
||: ⊓   ⊓   ⊓  :||
```

● For the △ shape use an open sound followed by two closed sounds:

 CD 60

● Alternatively, an open sound, followed by one closed, then another open sound:

 CD 61

● To create a relaxed feel some of the closed sounds may become almost silent, but still remain part of the rhythm and movement of the hands. This is achieved more through developing good listening than clapping technique. Emphasise the open sounds in the pattern and feel the exciting interplay of the cross rhythms produced.

WORKSHOP 3: USING RHYTHMIC SHAPES

● Write down a random order of △ and ⊓ shapes.

● Now, divide the group into two.

● Whilst one group maintains a continuous clapping pulse, the other group clap the written down pattern of △ and ⊓ shapes.

● Try experimenting with the placing of open and closed clapping strokes. Refer to the INSTRUMENT WORKSHOP on page 30.

● Use these rhythmic shapes to help understand the structure of time signatures, for example take two ⊓s and a △. Mix these three shapes in any order. Although there are always 7 claps to a group, or bar, there is a change in the emphasis of pulse, for example:

 CD 62 - 64

$$\frac{7}{8} \| : \quad \sqcap \quad \sqcap \quad \triangle \quad : \|$$
$$\frac{7}{8} \| : \quad \sqcap \quad \triangle \quad \sqcap \quad : \|$$
$$\frac{7}{8} \| : \quad \triangle \quad \sqcap \quad \sqcap \quad : \|$$

● If the group now adds a △ shape to these bars of 7 claps, we move into a 10/8 time signature (10 quaver, or eighth note, beats in a bar).

 CD 65 - 67

- Alternatively, by adding a ⊓ there is an interesting grouping of pulse for a 9/8 time signature:

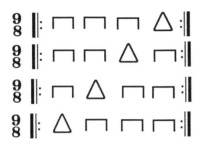

- Experiment by adding together groups of △ and ⊓ to discover new, exciting pulse patterns. Try writing out the examples in △ and ⊓ .

- To copy the clapping patterns used by the villagers of Botswana for *Celebration,* use the clapping part in the piano score. Again, one group can maintain a continuous clapping pulse whilst another group emphasises the rhythmic shapes using open and closed sounds. Listen to *Celebration* several times and clap with the backing band on CD.

- When the clapping group become more confident, allow each individual to experiment with the use of open and closed sounds. In *African Dances* these clapping patterns and sounds would not be dictated. It is both exciting and traditional for each individual in the clapping group to follow freely the melodic line, placing open and closed strokes where they 'feel' a natural emphasis or pulse. Listening is of paramount importance. The clapping must result from this listening, not from reading or dictation.

celebration

INSTRUMENT WORKSHOP

An open sound (o) is produced by **clapping** the flat fingers of one hand across the slightly cupped palm of the other hand:

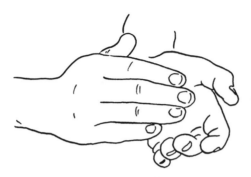

A closed sound (+) is produced by placing just the fingertips of the clapping hand onto the palm of the other hand:

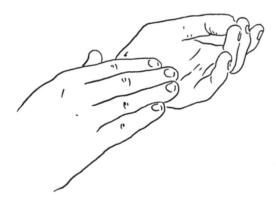

● For continuous rhythms the hands should not move far apart, feeling as though they are almost 'stuck' together. A relaxed feel is improved by slightly turning the cupped palm into the fingertips for the closed sound.

rainbow nation

Rainbow Nation is an arrangement of a Zulu song from South Africa. It uses a 7/8 time signature which is often found in African music. This exciting and flowing rhythmic pattern can be learnt through listening and repetition to create a 'feel' that is matched by dancing, singing, clapping and playing instruments.

 CD 72 *Rainbow Nation* – full performance

Using Pitch

One melody part is given, and can be sung or played on tuned percussion or melody instruments or sung. The piano score also includes chord symbols for guitar, etc.

Melody part for *Rainbow Nation* – see page 47.

 CD 73 *Rainbow Nation* – full backing only

RHYTHM ACCOMPANIMENT WORKSHOPS

Accompaniment to *Rainbow Nation* requires an understanding of the time signature 7/8, already encountered in *Celebration*. The use of such time signatures is commonplace in African songs. The workshops will develop an understanding of the internal structures of such time signatures. If students are introduced to music making without the structures of time signature and note values there is an opportunity to experiment with time and its divisions with open minds.

rhythm **1**
ACCOMPANIMENT
WORKSHOP

WORKSHOP 1: PULSE, 'FEEL' AND SUBDIVISION

● Get the group to stand in a large circle with eyes closed.

● The leader now plays a regular, slow pulse, preferably on a large resonant drum with a soft mallet (refer to the section on large drums on p.25). To ensure accuracy at this stage it may be helpful to use an electronic metronome with a light indication of pulse. Set the metronome to a pulse of about 40 beats per minute.

● Repeat the pulse many times so that the group begins to feel its regularity.

● Now ask the group to clap in unison with the pulse. Individuals will find it difficult to stay together with the group. With their eyes shut they are learning how hard it is to feel time without divisions.

- The leader now adds the following four-note subdivision on a drum to the pulse being clapped by the group. The leader may choose to think in a 7/8 time signature or use the rhythmic shapes explored in the *Celebration* workshops, whilst the group learns that their clap comes after the short note:

 CD 74

- It is important that the group now listens for an improved accuracy of the pulse and learns to relax whilst listening to the four-note rhythmic pattern.

- As individuals in the group become more comfortable, they can join in clapping the four note subdivision. Some in the group can continue with the pulse while others experiment with the subdivisions.

- The session must be continuous and relaxed. It is improved by constant repetition and allowing plenty of time for each stage to develop and become comfortable. The group must not feel challenged by rhythm and its subdivisions, but encouraged to discover its potential.

WORKSHOP 2: THE SOUND LIBRARY

- In the classroom virtually all objects and materials can be used to produce a range of sound textures and colours to become percussion instruments with their own library of sounds.

- Experiment with each 'instrument' to discover all possible techniques for creating sounds, then on a large sheet of paper note descriptions of each sound. Creative imagination should be encouraged to build a 'picture' of each sound in the library.

- It is important to be able to describe and, if possible, vocalise each sound. Think about the character, comparative pitch length, and relative volume of each sound.

- An individual from the group should now choose four distinct sounds from the sound library, for example:
  a) a low pitched, resonant sound
  b) a sound that sustains
  c) a loud, high pitched sound
  d) a crisp, yet quiet sound

It is possible that some sounds come from different ways of playing the same instrument.

- The instruments should be arranged so that all four sounds can be played by the one individual. There is a group learning process here of making decisions about the use of sticks or hands and the accessibility to instruments in performance.

- Now structure a performance of the four sounds using the four-note subdivision developed in Rhythm Accompaniment Workshop 1 in the following way:

 CD 75

Sounds: a b c d

It may help for the group to set up the drum and clapping framework before introducing the four new sounds.

- This is an example of using individual sounds 'melodically'. We can also discover how to combine sounds 'harmonically' as in the following example:

 CD 76

Try performing these patterns with the backing band on CD (CD 73).

WORKSHOP 3: ENSEMBLE

- Divide the group into four, each with instruments chosen from the sound library.

  Group 1 with low pitched resonant sounds

  Group 2 with sounds that sustain

  Group 3 with loud high pitched sounds

  Group 4 with crisp, yet quiet sounds

- First set up the pulse and clap the four-note subdivision with the whole workshop group, as described in Rhythm Accompaniment Workshop 1.

- When this has become relaxed and comfortable, group 1 can stop clapping in order to listen, then join with their low pitched, resonant sound as shown in Rhythm Accompaniment Workshop 2.

- Then, each group in turn can join the four-note subdivision. Each group plays its sound as part of the patterns learned in Rhythm Accompaniment Workshop 2.

- This group activity is developing part playing and ensemble work. Individuals in the ensemble can perform together because there is a common sense of pulse and rhythm. Each individual must listen to his/her sound as part of the common four-note subdivision.

- Individuals may experiment with different sounds and combinations within the four note pattern to find new 'melodic' shapes and 'harmonies'. Listen to each pattern for a long time. Keep the patterns that sound good and are comfortable and use as an accompaniment to *Rainbow Nation*.

INSTRUMENT WORKSHOP

- At the **drum kit** it is possible to make some simple guidelines to begin building some exciting patterns using combinations of △ and ⊓ . Refer to *Celebration* WORKSHOP 3: USING RHYTHMIC SHAPES on page 28.

- First, write out a pattern of shapes.

- Make a decision to play all ⊓ s within the pattern on foot bass drum and hand hi-hat together, and the △ s on cymbal and snare drum together. Play only the first down-beat of each shape and think or feel the remaining subdivisions.

- When these structures are comfortable and relaxed learn to move fluently through a range of time signatures, including 7/8 as an accompaniment to *Rainbow Nation*.

PART 1

Mavuto Megamix

PART 2

Mavuto Megamix

TUNE 'M'

5 TUNE 'A'

9 TUNE 'V'

13

17 TUNE 'U'

21

25 TUNE 'T'

29 TUNE 'O'

Mavuto Megamix

PART 2

BASS CLEF PART

Omusambwa Kwetsingoma

PART 1

Omusambwa Kwetsingoma

PART 2

Omusambwa Kwetsingoma

PART 2

25

28

31

Celebration

Celebration

PART 2

Celebration

PART 2

BASS CLEF PART

(play an octave lower ad lib.)

Rainbow Nation

CD contents

Mavuto Megamix

1	The whole piece, full performance
2	Tune 'M', parts 1 & 2 with backing
3	Tune 'A', parts 1 & 2 with backing
4	Tune 'V', parts 1 & 2 with backing
5	Tune 'U', parts 1 & 2 with backing
6	Tune 'T', parts 1 & 2 with backing
7	Tune 'O', parts 1 & 2 with backing
8	Tune 'M', part 2 with backing
9	Tune 'A', part 2 with backing
10	Tune 'V', part 2 with backing
11	Tune 'U', part 2 with backing
12	Tune 'T', part 2 with backing
13	Tune 'O', part 2 with backing
14	The whole piece, part 2 with backing
15	Tune 'M', part 1 with backing
16	Tune 'A', part 1 with backing
17	Tune 'V', part 1 with backing
18	Tune 'U', part 1 with backing
19	Tune 'T', part 1 with backing
20	Tune 'O', part 1 with backing
21	The whole piece, part 1 with backing
22	The whole piece, full backing only
23	Vocal phonetics *Gee-ya ka ka*
24	*Gee-ya ka ka*: patterns a, b, c & d (with backing)
25	*Gee-ya ka ka* with hand on body
26	*Gee-ya ka ka* with hand on body and footsteps
27	*Gung ka* with footsteps
28	*Gung ka* with footsteps and hand on body
29	Cymbal/snare drum/bass drum rhythmic pattern a)
30	Cymbal/snare drum/bass drum rhythmic pattern b)
31	*Gee-ya ka ka* with open/closed triangle: patterns a, b, c & d (with backing)
32	Open and closed cymbal

Omusambwa Kwetsingoma

33	The whole piece, full peformance
34	Tune 1, parts 1 & 2 with backing
35	Tune 2, parts 1 & 2 with backing

36	Tune 3, parts 1 & 2 with backing
37	Tune 4, parts 1 & 2 with backing
38	Tune 1, part 2 with backing
39	Tune 2, part 2 with backing
40	Tune 3, part 2 with backing
41	Tune 4, part 2 with backing
42	The whole piece, part 2 with backing
43	Tune 1, part 1 with backing
44	Tune 2, part 1 with backing
45	Tune 3, part 1 with backing
46	Tune 4, part 1 with backing
47	The whole piece, part 1 with backing
48	The whole piece, full backing only
49	Shaker rhythm with vocal phonetics *omusambwa kwetsingoma*
50	Voice patterns 1, 2, 3 & 4 (with backing)
51	Voice patterns 1, 2, 3 & 4 with drum (with backing)
52	Shaker rhythm
53	Open and closed drum sounds

Celebration

54	The whole piece, full performance
55	The whole piece, part 2 with backing
56	The whole piece, part 1 with backing
57	The whole piece, full backing only (with clapping)
58	The whole piece, full backing only (without clapping)
59	Clapping (open/closed): ⊓ shape
60	Clapping (open/closed/closed): △ shape
61	Clapping (open/closed/open): △ shape
62 – 64	Open/closed clapping: 7 claps to a bar
65 – 67	Open/closed clapping: 10 claps to a bar
66 – 71	Open/closed clapping: 9 claps to a bar

Rainbow Nation

72	The whole piece, full performance
73	The whole piece, full backing only
74	Clap and drum rhythm
75	Four drum sounds used as a 'melody'
76	Four drum sounds used 'harmonically'

Total running time: 52' 13"

All music written and performed by Paul Cameron. Piano: Richard King
Tracks 23 – 28, 31, 32, 49 – 53 & 59 – 71 recorded by Zig Zag Music Productions
(Engineer: Gareth Stuart. Producer: Richard King)
All other tracks engineered and produced at
Heritage Studio (Engineer: Greg Malcangi)